POETRY, PROSE & LOVE-NOTES

from the secret place

j. plummer

Copyright © J. Plummer 2023

All rights reserved. No part of this publication may be reproduced, distributed, or transmitted in any form or by any means, including photocopying, recording, or other electronic or mechanical methods, without the prior written permission of the publisher, except in the case of brief quotations embodied in critical reviews and certain other non-commercial uses permitted by copyright law.

✳ greenhill
https://greenhillpublishing.com.au/

Plummer, J. (author)
From The Secret Place
ISBN 978-1-923088-34-4
POETRY

Typeset Comorant Garamond 10/17
Illustrations by J.Plummer
Cover and book design by Green Hill Publishing

Contents

Autumn Leaves 1
The Secret Place 3
Valleys and Mountains 5
Though the Seasons Change 7
Present 8
His Eyes upon Me 9
There is a Word 10
He is Beauty Itself 11
A Poem about Some Things I do not know 12
Two that are One 13
Stars 14
Awaken 15
Eyes like an Ocean 17
Patiently 18
Freedom 19
In the Valley 21
Love doesn't need Persuading 22
And so it Begins 23
Deep Roots 24
The Right Path 25
Before the Sun 26
The Secret Garden of your Mind 28
Rock 29
Till This Love 31
Captivated 33

More than anything else	34
Indescribable	35
Things that remind me of you	36
Peace	37
Ashes to Gardens	39
Stillness	40
In that Moment I'll be your Wings	43
Held	44
Flow	45
Unveiled by Love	47
Cherry Blossom	48
Tears	49
Walking on Water	51
Home	53
Union	55
Lost and Found	57
Confetti	59
Eyes that say I Love You	61
Sunflower	63
Beauty in Believing	64
To Love You Is Who I Am	66
Yes	67
The Narrow Path	68
The Transformative Power of Incorruptible Love	70
Thank You	71

Autumn Leaves

Autumn leaves fall like the dreams of a heart that's been
  waiting too long...
But His love is like the spring.

from the secret place

The Secret Place

Under cover of night skies,
   adorned in celestial light,
   you meet me in the secret place

Where love reigns like a triumphant warrior
   clothed in glory
   more than a conqueror

Where mercies flow like gushing streams
   that run into the arms of the ocean of grace

Where hope springs up like wildflowers,
   resilient as they are beautiful

Where joy soars on the wings of the eagle,
   and mountains are moved by faith.

I sit and wait for your still, small voice,
   the flutter in my heart that tells me you are there …

Entering an intimacy that can't be undone;
   a place where two become one.
   A place where 'impossible' doesn't exist
   and the dreamer is free to dream.

Where wondrous visions come to life by Love's power and will.
   Where all fears are silenced,
   where all my doubts dissolve,
   and all that remains is the freedom found
   in love unconditional.

from the secret place

Valleys and Mountains

Valleys and mountains
and moments between
in quiet and secret,
and places unseen.
I search my heart to find you there;
your love speaks softly
like a child's prayer.
Full of hope
and everything true,
your tender love
will see me through.

Though the Seasons Change

Though the mountains crumble
   and the seasons change,
   in daylight or darkness
   your love remains.

Present

In twilight shades and the softest of lights,
   in silent frosts and still winter nights,
   in gentle rain and misty shrouds,
   in days that lag and in silver clouds,
   in times of loneliness and self-doubt,
   when the soul suffers a season of drought ...

You were present
   in a million subtle ways.
   I'm sorry for the times I didn't
   feel you there.

His Eyes upon Me

Like a marriage vow,
    with all the conviction and passion in the world,
    are His eyes upon me.
    Heavy with a promise
    and more intimate than a kiss.

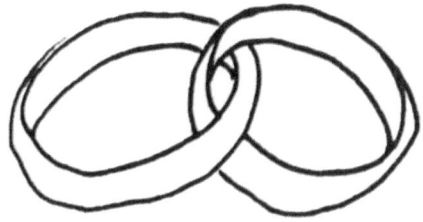

There is a Word

There is a word that describes all the joy, and wonder,
    and love that one could ever know...
It's *you*.

He is Beauty Itself

His beauty is unrivalled.
   Nothing compares ...

Not even a sunset in all its brilliance
   painting the heavens in the colours of love

Nor the open fields in the midst of spring
   dressed in flowers and adorned with new life

Nor the glistening waters of a moonlit sea
   that gently kisses satin shores.

He is beauty itself.
   The sun rises and sets with him.

A Poem about Some Things I do not know

There are many things I do not know –
   marvellous mysteries, too amazing to unravel.
   Who could explain them?

Like the way the birds serenade the rising sun,
   or the way spring beckons the blossoms to bloom,
   the eternal vastness of a starry sky,
   or the way my chest contracts when I think of you.

How your presence feels like home,
   and the way you make everything beautiful.

Two that are One

With a vow of everlasting love
  a destiny is assigned.
  A fate sealed by yielded hearts,
  Two souls are intertwined.
  In covenant love and passionate zeal,
  Two hearts become aligned,
  Too intimate to distinguish –
  Two that are one.
  A new identity defined.

Stars

I stare at the stars
   and ponder dreams that eluded me ...

Hand stretched up towards these
   sparkling spectacles, shining down on the earth
   like beacons of hope.

They shine right before my eyes,
   yet are forever beyond my reach.

But they're not beyond yours.

And as simple as an epiphany,
   the stars no longer elude me,
   for every promise and all my dreaming is fulfilled
   in your love.

Awaken

As the dawn breaks with silent beauty to softly
   wake the earth,
so He awakens my soul.

from the secret place.

Eyes like an Ocean

His eyes are like an ocean,
a beautiful, blue ocean of endless depth.
I am completely captivated.
Like a stone I sink into His eyes,
immersed in the tides of His affections –
welling-up, fervent, fierce and full of passion.
I want to sink right down,
down to the furthest depths of His heart.
I want to know Him in this way,
to uncover every hidden treasure,
every precious pearl and piece of priceless gold,
to seek out all there is to know,
just to be in awe.
So vast an ocean do these eyes reveal,
it would take all of eternity to explore
the many wonders of His heart.

Patiently

He struggles with words,
   but he feels safe in her arms,
     and each day she tries to love him more patiently.

Freedom

Freedom is knowing how much you love me.

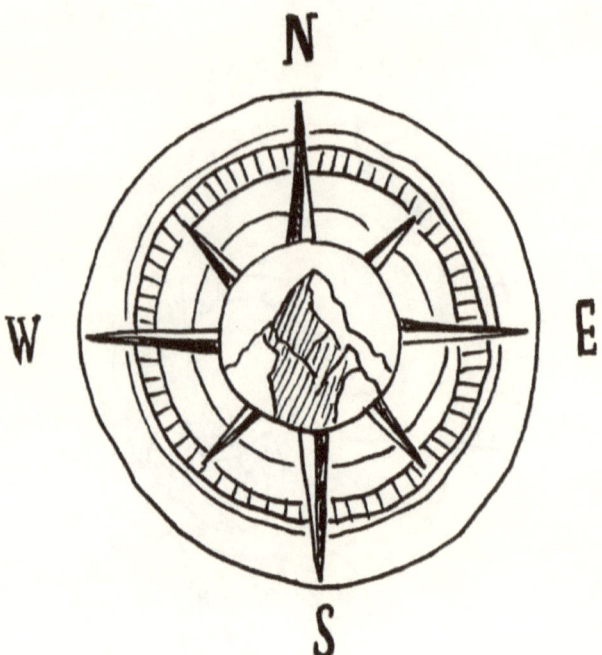

In the Valley

In valleys deep in shadow,
   far from the sun's warm reach,
   sights set on things above now faded,
   veiled by the falling rain.

Mountains masked by misty shrouds,
   majestic beauty drowned in grey;
   stairways of granite edges and these noble ledges
   now laden with rushing waterfalls.

With no way up and no way out,
   the valley seems a desperate place.
   But your love is a compass set in my heart,
   ensuring that I can never truly be lost.

As I remember to look within,
   the rain will pass,
   the path will become clear again,
   the courage to surmount mighty mountains will be found,
   and I will find my way back home.

Love doesn't need Persuading

Love doesn't need persuading,
    but it does require patience.
    It has mercy for mistakes,
    and is gentle and gracious.

Love is not naive,
    nor is it blind
    to the frailties and faults
    of mankind.

But Love's cause is greater than that of sin,
    and has power to bring forth the beauty within.

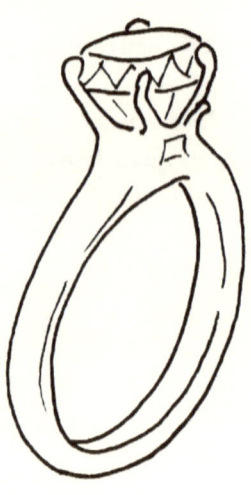

And so it Begins

I gaze into your eyes
   and all of a sudden,
     every impossibility seems possible.

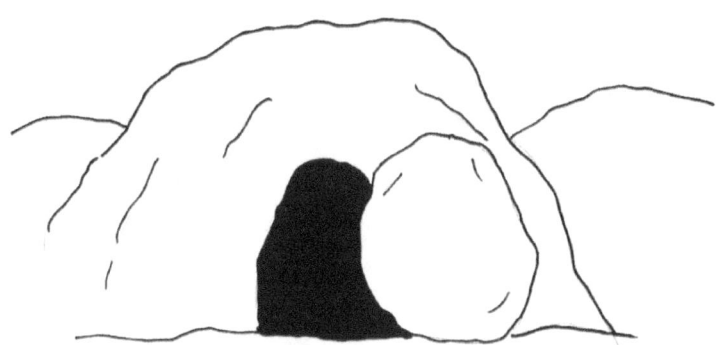

Deep Roots

Seeds hidden like cherished secrets –
   miracles waiting to bloom.
   Bury me deep within your heart,
   rooted and grounded in your perfect love.
   There I am safe, there I am secure.
   Roots that grow deep are not touched by the frost,
   nor easily ripped up.
   The deeper I know your love,
   the more I bloom and grow.

The Right Path

I know not where I'm going,
   nor how the pages of this story will read.
   I do not know the destinations
   to which this life will lead.

There's no telling how this moment
   will affect the aftermath.
   But as long as I am with you,
   I know I'm on the right path.

Before the Sun

Rustling my sheets,
   slowly I stir from a restless sleep.

I go to my window in a trance-like state,
   neither asleep nor awake.

I stare through dew-glazed glass,
   and watch a dull glow begin to rise
   over the hills.

I'm up before the sun …

Brooding over the world
   through the blurry glass
   unable to see clearly,
   unable to make sense of these
   shadows and silhouettes.

An ambiguous scene is set
   before my weary eyes.
   I move in closer to get a better look,
   But my breath clouds the vision
   all the more.

So I take a step back
   and wait.
   I surrender to the process and hold my peace,
   and allow the magnificence of the sun
   to fulfil its glorious cause.

Droplets begin to form and fall.
   They fall like tears
   that were once shed,
   Drip by drip
   until the view is unveiled.

Behold –
   the sun has conquered the hills
   and sits above the earth in golden splendour.

It beams through my window
   Like a spotlight upon me –
   as if to say,
   'It's your time, seize the day.'

The Secret Garden of your Mind

I forget time to know you more,
    lost in the garden of your imagination,
    wandering idly
    without a destination.

Thoughts like spring
    flower with inspiration;
    your beautiful mind transforms my heart
    with blossoming revelation.

Rock

Love is a rock.
   When storms came
   and winds blew,
   it did not move.

When the fire burnt through
   consuming all in its path,
   it remained ...
   the only thing left.

from the secret place

Till This Love

What was my life before this love?
   Any form of meaning or shadow or significance I might
   have known
   now seems incredibly infinitesimal.

Did I ever behold beauty?
   Did I ever feel warmth?
   Did I ever know what it is to be
   completely awestruck
   to the point where the heart surges with zeal
   stronger than death?

I see my face reflected in your eyes,
   and I've never felt so beautiful.
   Your heartbeat grounds me,
   words leave your lips like life itself.
   Your presence is a fountain for my thirsty soul.

Waking to you each morning is like the
   first day of spring,
   and every kiss goodnight is a
   remedy for this lovesickness.

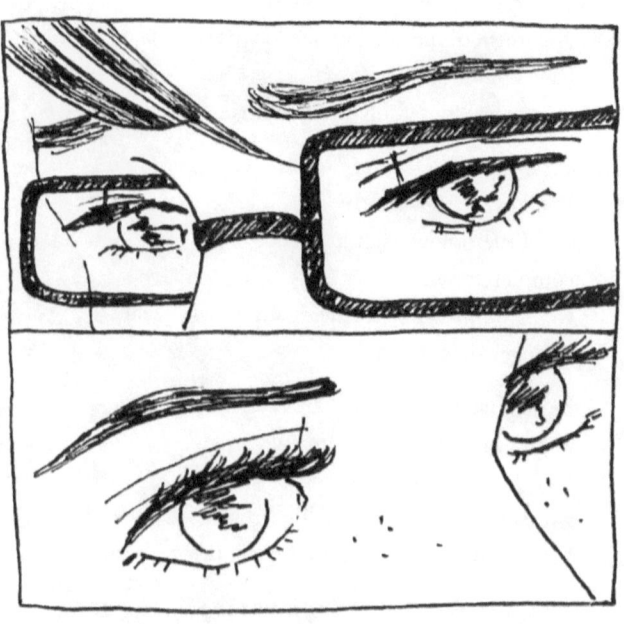

Captivated

Captivated and bound,
   in your eyes I am found.
   Focus so intense,
   breaking my defence.
   Eyes that see straight through,
   tender and true,
   searching each component,
   eternity in a moment.
   Heart beats recklessly.
   Words whispered breathlessly
   spoken without hesitation –
   words of adoration.
   Words of love I receive,
   words of love I believe.
   My heart, your love has healed.
   To your love I yield.

More than anything else

There's far more than meets the eye.
  Let me tell you what I see ...
  Your heart is beauty itself to me.

And everything that flows from it
  means more than the celestial heavens
  or the radiant sun,
    and everything else that life centres around.

Indescribable

There are some moments you can't put into words.
This is one of them.

Things that remind me of you

Things that remind me of you …
    Where the undulating mountain range
    meets the heavenly blue,
    the beginning of spring
    making all things new.
    Early in the morning
    When the sun breaks through,
    the cherry tree blossoms
    with their captivating hue.
    Secret gardens
    and sun-kissed dew …
    Everything beautiful
    reminds me of you.

Peace

There is no greater peace than this:
  my lover is mine and I am His.

Ashes to Gardens

Time may have left a ruinous trail of things I wish I could erase,
but your love transcends time,
Permeating every part of all there ever was, and all there
ever is, and all there ever will be.
It reaches the furthest corners of my being and very
existence.
It touches every hidden and secret place.
It heals my past and illuminates the way forward.
It gives me hope and purpose, and renews my reason for being.
It casts out my fears, and banishes the dark.
It draws back the curtains of my mind and floods it with
warm healing light.
Like the sun, it springs forth life from the soil of my soul,
and turns these ashes into gardens.

Stillness

Stillness
A sacred place
where my heart is steady,
my mind at peace.

In stillness I wait –
I wait for the one
who loves my soul.

In stillness He comes
gently,
like a feather adrift,
making a slow descent
in silence.

I feel the soft touch
of His presence,
and I am weightless.

Like a feather adrift
I am swept up,
making a slow ascent
on the winds of His affections.

He carries me gently
into the sacred place
of His heart.

Waiting for me
in stillness.

from the secret place

In that Moment
I'll be your Wings

Accept my kiss upon your brow,
   and allow me to avow
   things more true and deep,
   and a promise I pray to keep ...

Which is to love you without ceasing,
   and in doing so releasing
   you to the destiny to which you are called,
   to fulfil and be enthralled
   in the adventure awaiting you,
   and to empower you to do
   all that is in your heart,
   and I promise to do my part.

And as you approach destiny's ledge
   I'll hold your hand and keep my pledge.
   In that moment I'll be your wings,
   and help you rise above the things
   that keep you from flying,
   with love that's edifying.

Held

He held me so close
that we became one.

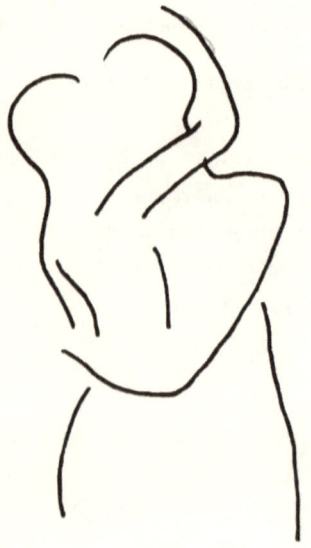

Flow

Creativity is like a river; it must be allowed to flow.
   Otherwise it becomes stagnant, it doesn't produce life,
   and it can make the heart sick.
Use the gifts

Unveiled by Love

As a groom unveils the face of his beloved bride,
   You have unveiled me right down to the very sheaths of
   my nerves and sinew.
   You have unveiled me right down to all that holds my
   being together.
   You have unveiled me right down to my very core,
   with eyes that see through the deep blue in mine,
   through to the sacred light within.

Like a rose embowered by its own foliage,
   You push past it all to marvel at the beauty.
   You know me so completely,
   inside and out.
   You know every shade of autumn in my auburn locks,
   to the love language of my heart.

And in knowing all there is to know –
   without secrets or pretence –
   still you only see the most lovely thing
   that one could ever behold.

Cherry Blossom

I am the cherry blossom
    and you are the spring.

You cause the delicate petals
    of my heart to unfurl.

Then at the faintest breath from your lips,
    I fall …

Floating like a kiss on a breeze,
    swept up in the winds of your love.

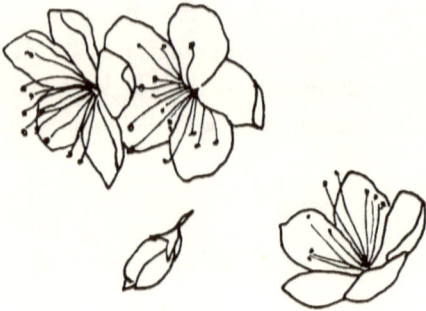

Tears

These eyes have leaked hope and seeped sorrow.
   From them have come splashes of joy
   and drops of disappointment.

Yet there hasn't been a tear I've shed that you didn't feel.

Not one has gone unnoticed,
   not one lost,
   not one forgotten.

You know each one,
   you know their story,
   you know them the way a lover knows the innermost depths
   of their beloved.

You know them like a secret,
   you know them like your own heart's song.

And you were always there to meet each one
   with open arms, and a heart that aches
   to love me a hundred times greater
   for every tear shed.

Walking on Water

In water you're weightless.
   You idly make a slow descent
   without quite reaching the ocean floor,
   stuck somewhere in-between, in limbo,
   dragged around by the tide,
   living day by day
   at the mercy of the waves,
   welling up and rolling over.

Sometimes the sea is gentle,
   and you rise and fall with each
   subtle swell.
   Sometimes you get caught up
   in the violent whitewash
   thrashing you around,
   losing all sense of direction,
   losing all sense of yourself.

But since that day,
   you came into my life.
   I now walk upon the water –
   the waves beneath my feet.

Home

He is my safest place,
    and my greatest adventure.
    He is the voice of love
    and destiny.
    He is the confidence to do the impossible,
    and the giver of dreams.
    He is the journey,
    and He is home.

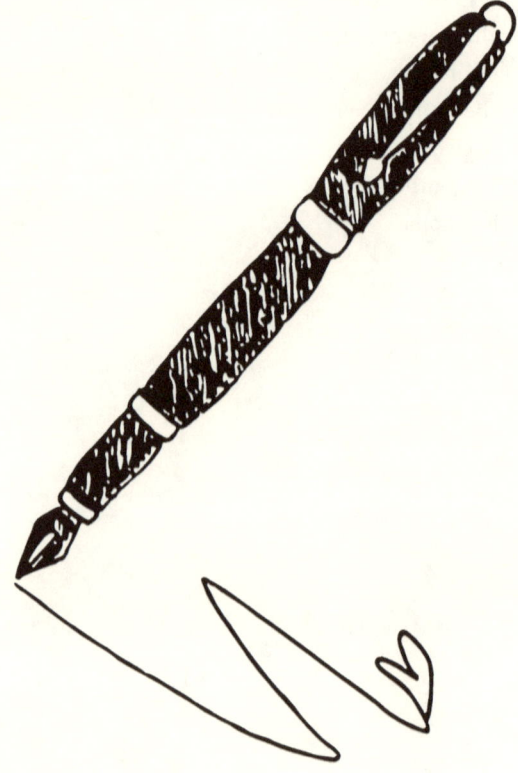

from the secret place

Union

Ink embellishes the page with cherished sentiments,
   a union of artistry inspired by
   passionate love.

The key perfectly formed to fit the right lock
   reaches the innermost parts of her lover,
   causing him to open the door
   to an entire world of wonder.

Waves clasp one another in a dramatic rush,
   like lovers reunited
   after being apart.

The morning sun caresses the earth
   like warm hands on rosy cheeks,
   and moonbeams kiss the sea
   in the secrecy of night.

Nothing in this world seems single.
   By divine design unions are
   destined to be.

But of all the marvellous unions in this world,
   none are more complete
   or beautiful
   or powerful
   than that of you and me.

from the secret place

Lost and Found

Lost,
   a snowflake
   in the desert,
   destined for the mountain top,
   but found myself on desolate ground.

There I lay
   staring up at the stars that seem so far away,
   melting slowly,
   Feeling every last hope slip through the cracks.

But then
   the voice of love spoke with solidifying power,
   and said,
   'I'm here to take you home,
   to the mountain top
   where you and I belong.'

from the secret place

Confetti

You are like confetti at a wedding,
   bursting with colour like glistening sequence,
   soft and sweet as rose petals.

You are a sense of celebration.
   You are the air of anticipation.
   You breathe in dreams and exhale joy.

You are the essence of things hoped for,
   and the substance of things unseen.

From your smile flows breathless warmth,
   and in your eyes, an eternal reassurance,
   and a promise ...
   that there is nothing in the whole world
   that you adore more than me.

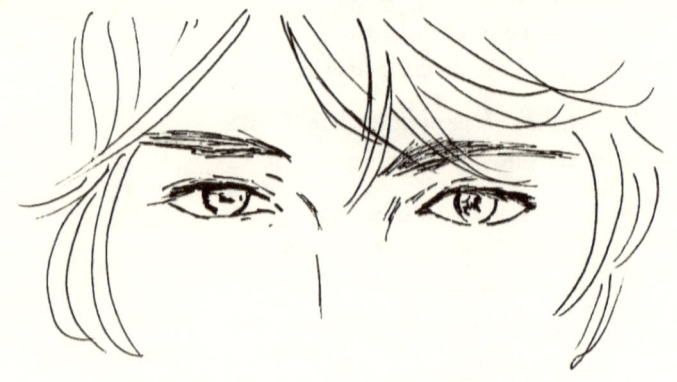

Eyes that say I Love You

He has eyes that reach me
   before he takes a step,
   eyes that embrace me
   before I'm in his arms,
   eyes that kiss me
   before his lips meet mine,
   eyes that say *I love you*
   before the words are spoken.

from the secret place

Sunflower

The sunflower turns her face to the sun.
   She is moved by the warmth of His love.
   She looks not in any other direction.
   There is nothing else that can captivate her attention.
   She seeks no other substance,
   for all she desires
   is found in her sun.

And when the night comes,
   she looks to the east
   anticipating the rise of her only love.
   With long-suffering devotion, she waits for Him,
   looking nowhere else,
   so as not to miss a moment of His radiance.

And just like the sunflower,
   I am only moved by one and one alone.
   For I am she,
   And you are my sun.

Beauty in Believing

There is beauty in believing.
    It causes the soul to flourish
    and strengthens the heart.
    It is the beginning of inspiration
    and the birthplace of miracles.

There is nothing more mysterious
    than the transformative nature of the believing heart.
    It shifts the tides of destiny
    and stirs the sea of eternity
    like a stone dropped in still waters,
    creating a ripple effect of boundless reach.

It's the tree that bears fruit out of season,
    it's the bird that defies the law of gravity,
    it's the unseen power in a promise,
    it's the anchor in the waves,
    it's the unbidden song of a poet
    immersed in the light of revelatory thought.

It's the lamp that marks home,
   it's the compass when lost,
    it's the small voice that whispers *Don't give up*
   when all seems too much.

It moves mountains and parts seas.
   And because you believe in me
   and I in you,
   there is nothing on the earth
   we cannot do.

To Love You Is Who I Am

To love you is who I am,
   and to not love you –
   I wouldn't know how.

But if it were possible,
   I would not be me –

I'd be like a bird that could no longer fly,
   or a star that could not shine,
   a flower without a fragrance,
   a branch without a vine.

And just like that branch cut from the vine,
   my life would bear no fruit,
   and my heart would wither.

Without love to abide in
   what then would I be,
   what would be left of me?

Yes

When the world said *No*, you said *Yes*.
And that's all that matters.

The Narrow Path

I journey down the forest path
   until the path diverges,
   but not equally.

One path is wide and the other is narrow.
   The wide path goes down into the valley
   with an effortless decline,
   easy and accessible –
   the path most travelled,
   evident by its lack of growth.
   You can see a long way ahead.
   There is a sense of certainty,
   yet I'm confronted by its vastness,
   open like a wide, gaping mouth
   ready to swallow me up.

The narrow path goes uphill,
   a steep arduous climb.
   I would have to contend with the undergrowth;
   abundant with life, it twists and turns.
   There is not much to see beyond the early sharp bend.
   It imposes the unknown,
   yet it calls to me
   like a promise made to myself
   that I must keep.

I stand at the fork of two destinies calling,
   torn between my flesh and my spirit.

The flesh yearns for the wide path,
   with its promise of effortless self-gratification.

But my spirit desires the narrow path.
   With discerning power it compels me to believe
   I can be greater,
   That my life must rise towards heaven.

So ...
   with one final deep breath,
   I prepare for the climb.

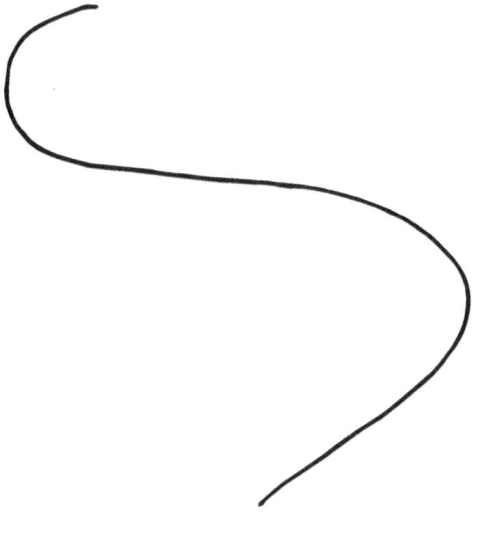

The Transformative Power of Incorruptible Love

I loved you out of brokenness; I loved you out of need.
I tried to love you from an empty cup and because of that,
 I failed to love you well.
Yet all along you were concealing an incorruptible dream,
 a dream for us, a dream for me.
My shortcomings could not shake you.
You remained consistent throughout.
You never looked upon me with disappointed eyes,
 you never spoke to me from a broken heart.
You did not lose the disposition of perfect love.
And because I couldn't change that,
you had the power to save me.

Thank You

For all the stars that whispered
  Miracles still happen,
    and for all the flowers that reminded me
    there is beauty if you look

For the sun that rises each morning,
  and because it rises, so do I,
    even on the days I have no strength

For the rain that heals the earth,
  that prophetically speaks with each drop,
    declaring there is healing for every tear

For the moon that guides me in the dark,
  and for the soothing lullaby of the ocean shore,
    for the thunder's roar
    inspiring the power
    you have placed inside my heart

Thank you.

www.ingramcontent.com/pod-product-compliance
Lightning Source LLC
La Vergne TN
LVHW090042080526
838202LV00046B/3918